U.S. HISTORY IN REVIEW

The Civil War

SADIE SILVA

Enslow Publishing

Please visit our website, www.enslow.com. For a free color catalog of all our high-quality books, call toll free 1-800-398-2504 or fax 1-877-980-4454.

Library of Congress Cataloging-in-Publication Data
Names: Silva, Sadie, author.
Title: The Civil War / Sadie Silva.
Description: Buffalo, New York : Enslow Publishing, [2023] | Series: U.S. history in review | Includes index.
Identifiers: LCCN 2022021883 (print) | LCCN 2022021884 (ebook) | ISBN 9781978529083 (library binding) | ISBN 9781978529069 (paperback) | ISBN 9781978529090 (ebook)
Subjects: LCSH: United States–History–Civil War, 1861-1865–Juvenile literature.
Classification: LCC E468 .S54 2023 (print) | LCC E468 (ebook) | DDC 973.7–dc23/eng/20220510
LC record available at https://lccn.loc.gov/2022021883
LC ebook record available at https://lccn.loc.gov/2022021884

Published in 2023 by
Enslow Publishing
2544 Clinton Street
Buffalo, NY 14224

Portions of this work were originally authored by Peter Castellano and published as *The Civil War*. All new material in this edition authored by Sadie Silva.

Designer: Leslie Taylor
Editor: Caitie McAneney

Photo credits: Cover, p. 17 Everett Collection/Shutterstock.com; series art (grunge flag) Andrey Kuzmin/Shutterstock.com; series art (stamp icon) Stocker_team/Shutterstock.com; series art (font) santstock/Shutterstock.com; p. 5 Everett Collection/Shutterstock.com; p. 7 https://commons.wikimedia.org/wiki/File:Original_1861_Map_of_the_Confederate_States,_Harper%27s_Weekly,_February_23,_1861.jpg; p. 8 Everett Collection/Shutterstock.com; p. 9 Everett Collection/Shutterstock.com; p. 10 Radomir Rezny/Shutterstock.com; p. 11 https://commons.wikimedia.org/wiki/File:The_Civil_War_-_the_national_view_(1906)_(14739688936).jpg; p. 13 Tom Hillmeyer/Shutterstock.com; p. 15 (photo) Everett Collection/Shutterstock.com; p. 15 (stamp) spatuletail/Shutterstock.com; p. 19 https://commons.wikimedia.org/wiki/File:First_Battle_of_Bull_Run_Kurz_%26_Allison.jpg; p. 20 https://commons.wikimedia.org/wiki/File:Ironclads_battle_7.jpg; p. 21 https://commons.wikimedia.org/wiki/File:Battle between the Monitor and Merrimac-fought March 9th 1862 at Hampton Roads, near Norfolk, Va. LCCN91482238.jpg; p. 23 https://commons.wikimedia.org/wiki/File:J._S._Smith_%26_Co._copy_of_the_Emancipation_Proclamation.tif; p. 25 Abel Tumik/Shutterstock.com; p. 26 Everett Collection/Shutterstock.com; p. 27 Everett Collection/Shutterstock.com; p. 29 Everett Collection/Shutterstock.com.

Printed in the United States of America

CPSIA compliance information: Batch #CWENS23: For further information, contact Enslow Publishing at 1-800-398-2504.

Contents

Words in the glossary appear in **bold** *the first time they are used in the text.*

War Between the States

Less than 100 years after winning **independence**, the United States was at war again. This time, two parts of the country were at war with each other. In the American Civil War, the Union (Northern states) fought against the Confederacy (Southern states).

Learn More

The American Civil War took place between 1861 and 1865. Sometimes it's called the "war between the states."

A Country Divided

A civil war is a fight between two groups in a country. In the new United States, Northern states and Southern states had many differences. The South's **economy** was based on farming. The North's economy was mostly based on factories.

map of Confederate States, 1861

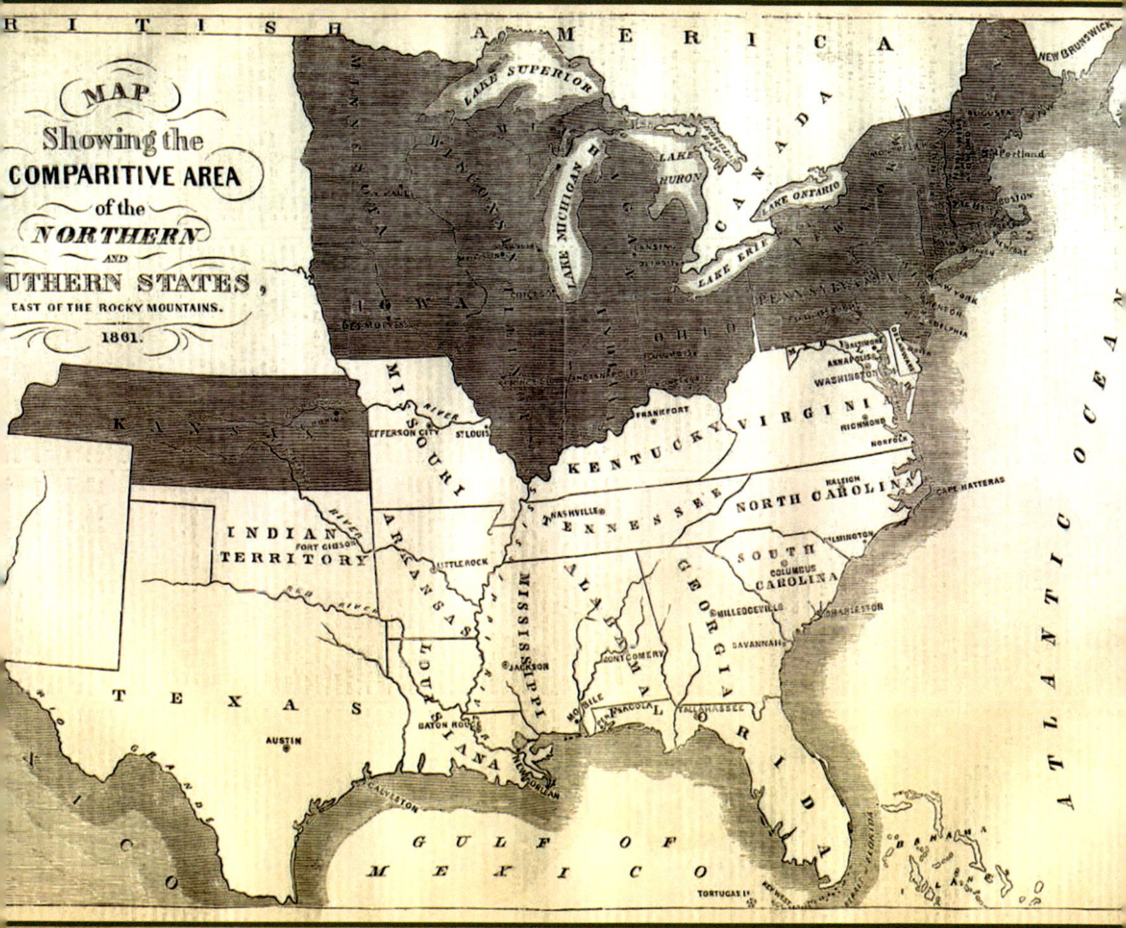

In 1828, Congress passed a high tax the South felt only helped the North. A lower tax passed in 1832, but South Carolina voted to **nullify** the law anyway.

The South believed states' rights included the ability to nullify federal, or national, laws. The battle over states' governmental powers included other matters, too, such as slavery. The South's economy depended on slavery, while the North's didn't.

young enslaved person during the Civil War, 1863

auction of enslaved people in Richmond, Virginia, 1856

Learn More

Slavery had existed in the colonies, and then states, since 1619. By the 1800s, many Northerners wanted slavery **abolished** for the whole country.

Neither the North nor the South wanted the other's ideas to spread to new U.S. states. The Missouri Compromise of 1820 banned slavery north of Missouri's southern border. It allowed Missouri to join the nation as a slave state and Maine as a free state.

This map shows the result of the Missouri Compromise of 1820.

Learn More

in 1854, the Kansas-Nebraska Act allowed Kansas and Nebraska to choose whether they would be slave or free states. As a result, Northerners and Southerners fought in the new states.

A Major Election

The presidential election of 1860 was a turning point for the country. Abraham Lincoln ran for president as a Republican, a group against slavery that wanted to keep the country together. When he won, the North controlled both the presidency and Congress.

Lincoln Memorial, Washington, DC

Learn More

Abraham Lincoln won the 1860 election despite not even being on the **ballot** in the South! The Southern states felt they had lost their say in the federal government.

Leaving the United States

Seven Southern states seceded, or left, the United States after the 1860 election. They formed the Confederate States of America. By April 1861, four more states had joined them. But the rest of the world didn't recognize the Confederacy as an independent country.

Learn More

Jefferson Davis was chosen as the president of the Confederacy. However, the world still saw Abraham Lincoln as the leader of the United States.

Strengths on Both Sides

The Union had many strengths in the war. They had the U.S. Army, more people, and more railroads. However, the South had skilled military leaders. Furthermore, they were fighting for a major cause—independence. The Confederates also fought on land they knew well.

Battle of Shiloh, 1862

Learn More

Much of the fighting of the Civil War would happen in the Southern states of Virginia and Tennessee. Confederates were **defending** their homes.

Battles Begin

The American Civil War began with the Battle of Fort Sumter in April 1861 in Charleston, South Carolina. By July, both sides had armies. By the end of 1861, fighting had broken out in Virginia, Maryland, and Pennsylvania. In the West, battles broke out along the Mississippi River.

Learn More

On July 21, 1861, the Confederates and the Union army fought the First Battle of Bull Run in Manassas Junction, Virginia. The Confederate army won this first major land battle of the war.

First Battle of Bull Run, 1861

In March 1862, the two sides fought the Battle of Hampton Roads by sea. The Confederacy's *Merrimack* and the Union's *Monitor* were ships covered in iron. When they fought in March 1862, neither ship truly won the battle.

Monitor vs. *Merrimack*, 1862

Monitor vs. *Merrimack*, 1862

Learn More

In 1862, the Union won at the Battles of Shiloh and Antietam. The Confederates won the Second Battle of Bull Run and the Battle of Fredericksburg.

Freedom for All

Slavery was a major issue in the Civil War. Feeling **encouraged** by the Union's win at Antietam, President Lincoln felt it was time to deal with slavery. In 1863, the Emancipation Proclamation freed all the slaves in Confederate states. Many Black soldiers joined the Union army.

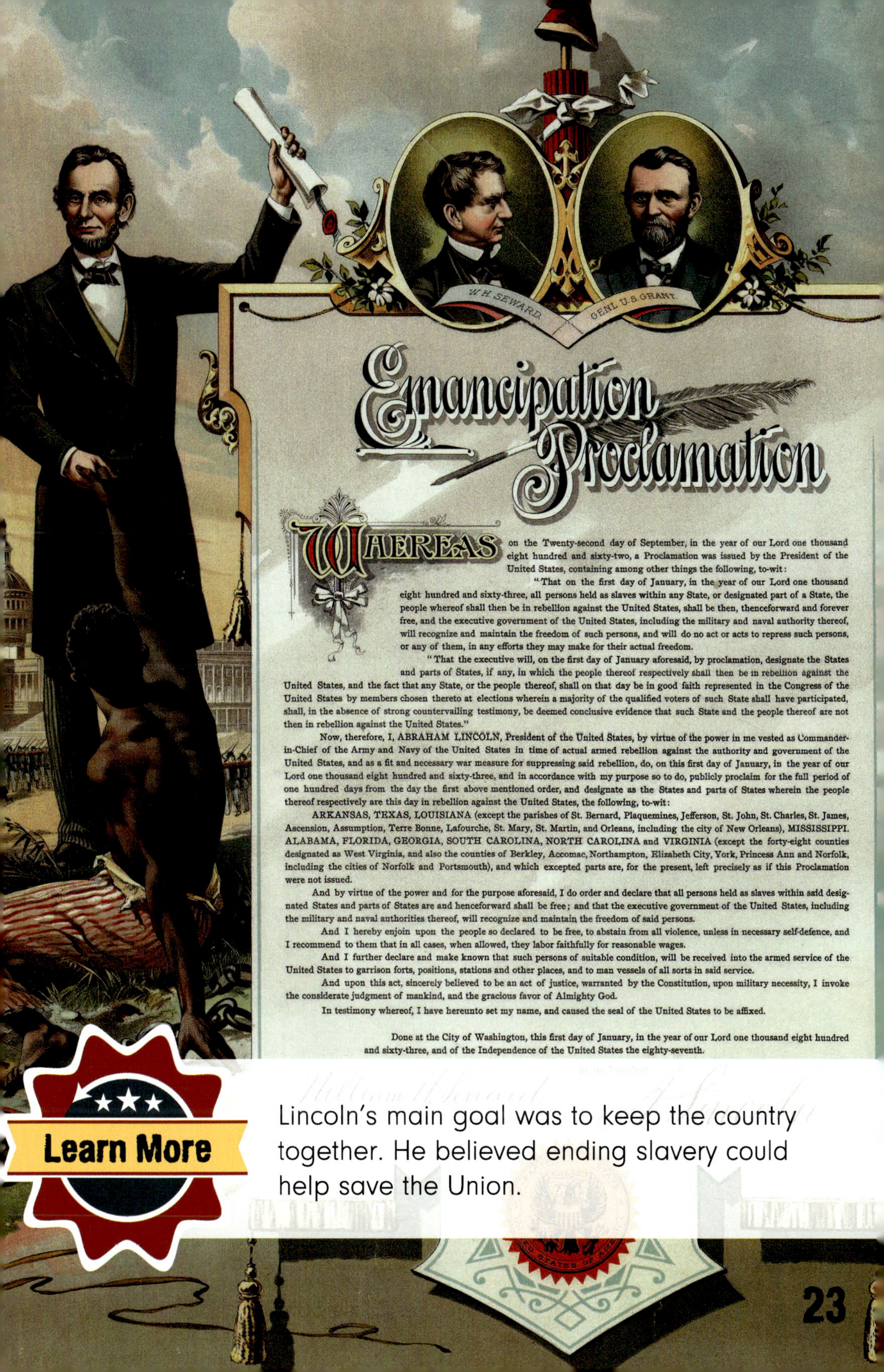

Learn More

Lincoln's main goal was to keep the country together. He believed ending slavery could help save the Union.

Union Victories

The Battle of Gettysburg in July 1863 was the bloodiest battle of the American Civil War. The Union army stopped Confederate forces from **invading** the North in Gettysburg, Pennsylvania. Right after, Ulysses S. Grant led the Union army as they won control of the Mississippi River.

Ulysses S. Grant, $50 bill

Learn More

Ulysses S. Grant commanded the Union army beginning in March 1864. In 1869, this war hero became the nation's 18th president.

The Battle of Gettysburg was a turning point in the war. The Union continued to overtake Confederate forces into 1864. In June 1864, Grant began a **siege** on Petersburg, Virginia. By 1865, Confederate general Robert E. Lee had few men and supplies and gave up Petersburg.

Abraham Lincoln, 1862

Learn More

Abraham Lincoln won reelection in 1864. However, he was shot and killed on April 14, 1865.

Battle of Gettysburg, 1863

The End of the War

The American Civil War ended in 1865. On April 9, 1865, Lee **surrendered** in Appomattox Court House, Virginia. All other Confederate forces surrendered soon after. After the war, Southern states rejoined the Union. This was a long journey for the South, a period called **Reconstruction**.

surrender in Appomattox Court House, 1865

Learn More

Reconstruction lasted until 1877. With slavery gone, Southern states created "black codes" that led to injustice and **violence** against Black Americans.

Timeline

1820
The Missouri Compromise bans slavery north of Missouri's southern border.

1854
The Kansas-Nebraska Act is passed.

1860
Abraham Lincoln is elected president.

April 1861
Eleven states have seceded from the United States.

July 21, 1861
The First Battle of Bull Run is the first major land battle of the war.

March 1862
The Battle of Hampton Roads occurs.

January 1, 1863
Abraham Lincoln issues the Emancipation Proclamation.

July 1863
The Battle of Gettysburg is fought in Gettysburg, Pennsylvania.

June 1864
Grant leads a Union siege on Petersburg, Virginia.

April 9, 1865
Lee surrenders in Appomattox Court House, Virginia.

April 14, 1865
Abraham Lincoln is shot and killed.

Glossary

abolish: To do away with.

ballot: A sheet of paper listing names of those running for office and used for voting.

defend: To guard against harm.

economy: The money made in an area and how it is made.

encourage: To give hope to.

independence: Freedom from outside control.

invade: To enter a place to take it over.

nullify: To do away with a law.

Reconstruction: The period from 1865 to 1877 in which southern states rejoined the United States after the American Civil War.

siege: The use of military to surround an area or building in order to capture it.

surrender: To give up.

violence: The use of force to harm someone.

For More Information

Books

Shea, Therese. *Abraham Lincoln and Frederick Douglass.* New York, NY: Gareth Stevens Publishing, 2022.

Rumsch, BreAnn. *Ulysses S. Grant.* Minneapolis, Minnesota: Abdo Publishing, 2021.

Website

American Civil War
www.dkfindout.com/us/history/american-civil-war/
Discover more about key battles, figures, and issues during the American Civil War.

Publisher's note to educators and parents: *Our editors have carefully reviewed these websites to ensure that they are suitable for students. Many websites change frequently, however, and we cannot guarantee that a site's future contents will continue to meet our high standards of quality and educational value. Be advised that students should be closely supervised whenever they access the internet.*

Index